PUBLISHER	Joseph R. DeVarennes
PUBLICATION DIRECTOR	Kenneth H. Pearson
MANAGING EDITOR	Valerie Wyatt
SERIES ADVISOR	Merebeth Switzer
SERIES CONSULTANT	Michael Singleton
CONSULTANTS	Ross James
	Kay McKeever
	Dr. Audrey N. Tomera
ADVISORS	Roger Aubin
	Robert Furlonger
	Gaston Lavoie
EDITORIAL SUPERVISOR	Jocelyn Smyth
PRODUCTION MANAGER	Ernest Homewood
PRODUCTION ASSISTANTS	Penelope Moir
	Brock Piper

EDITORS

Katherine Farris   Anne Minguet-Patocka
Sandra Gulland   Sarah Reid
Cristel Kleitsch   Cathy Ripley
Elizabeth MacLeod   Eleanor Tourtel
Pamela Martin   Karin Velcheff

PHOTO EDITORS   Bill Ivy
   Don Markle

DESIGN   Annette Tatchell
CARTOGRAPHER   Jane Davie
PUBLICATION ADMINISTRATION   Kathy Kishimoto
   Monique Lemonnier

ARTISTS   Marianne Collins   Greg Ruhl
   Pat Ivy   Mary Theberge

This series is approved and recommended
by the Federation of Ontario Naturalists.

Canadian Cataloguing in Publication Data

Dingwall, Laima, 1953-
  Bison

(Getting to know—nature's children)
Includes index.
ISBN 0-7172-1925-9

1. Bison—Juvenile literature.
I. Title. II. Series.

QL737.U53D56 1985   j599.73'58   C85-098704-0

Have you ever wondered . . .

Meet the most magnificent animal in North America. It is the mighty bison, or buffalo, as it is often mistakenly called.

The bison is the largest land animal on this continent. It is also as much a part of the Old West as Jesse James and Buffalo Bill. It is even mentioned in an old song that begins: "Oh, give me a home where the buffalo roam . . ." That song is called "Home on the Range." And that is exactly where the bison makes its home.

Bison are found primarily on plains and prairies.

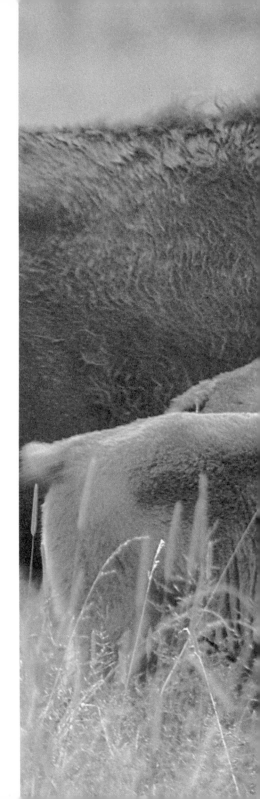

Playtime

Young bison love to play. They kick up their back legs and bound across fields in a bison version of tag, or they butt heads and shove each other in a pretend battle. Sometimes a young bison might even play-fight with a springy tree branch. It shoves the branch away with its head, only to have it bounce back again for another shove.

This play has a serious side. As they frolic, the young bison are strengthening their muscles and learning the skills that they will need to defend themselves and be part of the herd.

These twins are careful to stay close to their mother.

Meet the Relatives

If the bison had a family reunion for all its North American relatives, who would come? Its cousins, of course: the Mountain Goat, Muskox, Bighorn Sheep and Dall's Sheep.

All these animals have a number of things in common. They all chew cud. This means that these animals eat now and chew later, when they have more time. The bison and its relatives also have split hoofs for feet and horns on their heads. And none of these animals has any top front teeth.

Many people call the bison a buffalo. But that is not correct. Buffalo live in Asia and Africa, and they are not even related to bison. Buffalo and bison are different in two ways. Buffalo do not have a huge hump on their back like bison have. And buffalo have 13 pairs of ribs, while bison have 14 pairs.

Despite its size a bison eats only one-third as much as a domestic cow.

Here a Bison, There a Bison

There are two types of bison in North America: the Wood Bison and the Plains Bison. It is easy to tell the two apart. The Wood Bison is larger and it has a much darker and woollier coat than its cousin. The Wood Bison, as you may have guessed from its name, lives in wooded areas. For the most part, these wooded areas are farther north than the open plains where the Plains Bison lives.

Big, Bigger, Biggest

The bison is the biggest land animal in North America. A full-grown male Wood Bison stands between one and a half and two metres (5-6.5 feet) tall at the shoulder—about the same height as an adult man. But unlike a man, a bison tips the scale at between 635 and 1000 kilograms (1400-2200 pounds). That is about the same weight as 10 adult men put together. Female bison are slightly smaller.

Opposite page:

Wood Bison.

Warm, Shaggy Coats

The bison's head, hump and forelegs are covered with thick, shaggy chocolate brown fur. Actually this fur coat is two coats in one. Close to the bison's body is a layer of thick underfur. This traps body-warmed air next to the bison's skin. Another coat of guard hairs sheds water and keeps out wind.

In spring, the bison starts getting ready for the hot weather to come by shedding its warm winter coat. Its lighter summer coat takes about two months to grow in.

The bison's hind quarters and legs are covered with shorter, straight coppery brown fur. And a long thick beard grows from the bison's chin.

Head-to-head combat.

See, Smell and Hear

You would have to be very clever—or lucky—to sneak up on a bison. The bison's big, soft brown eyes can spot something move up to three-quarters of a kilometre (half a mile) away. Its wide, flat nose can pick up a scent up to one and a half kilometres (1 mile) away. And those two round fuzzy ears can hear twigs crackle and snap some 150 metres (500 feet) away.

Keen senses are particularly important to the Plains Bison. They must be able to sense danger quickly because they have no place to hide from their enemies. Their only protection is to turn and fight or run away.

All bison have long shaggy beards.

Horn Headgear

Both the male and female bison have horns. They use their horns to defend themselves against enemies and in fights with other bison.

Bison horns are very sharp and very long. A full-grown male may have horns as long as 38 centimetres (15 inches). To keep its horns sharp and polished, the bison rubs them against trees. If there are no trees nearby, it will use anything that sticks up from the ground: a boulder, a bush or a sapling. Even a mound of dirt or a pile of snow in winter will do.

A Relaxing Rub

The bison not only rubs its horns against things; it also gets its head, shoulders and sides into the rubbing act. At times, especially during the spring and summer when it has shed its winter coat, it seems to go rub crazy. No wonder. That is the time of year when biting insects are worst. Rubbing not only helps stop insect pests from biting, it also keeps them from laying their eggs on the bison's back.

Sometimes bison even roll around on the ground to rub their backs. When this happens, dust flies everywhere as they flop back and forth. As they roll around a bowl-shaped hole is flattened out in the dust. These holes, called "buffalo wallows," are sometimes four and a half metres (15 feet) across.

Besides getting rid of insects, wallowing also helps bison rub off any loose patches of fur. And now scientists think that it might also be the bison's way of relaxing and getting rid of tension.

Opposite page:

A bison in its mud wallow.

Tail End

At the end of the bison's tail is a tassle of long hair which makes a very good fly swatter. When the bison swishes its tail back and forth, it discourages any flies and other insects from biting or laying their eggs on its hindquarters.

At rest

If you want to know what a bison is thinking, look at its tail. When the bison's tail is hanging down, the bison is calm. But when its tail is sticking up into the air—beware—this means that it is upset and may even charge.

Alarmed

Getting Around

Do not be fooled by the bison's huge, bulky body. It can run as fast as a car on a city street—for short distances. The bison is also a fine swimmer. It is comfortable in water and swims dog-paddle style with only its head and hump showing.

The bison is also well equipped for mountain climbing. With its sharp hoofs and strong legs, it can climb up and down rocky mountains with ease.

Bison on the Move

People once thought that bison spent the spring and summer grazing in the northern parts of their range, then migrated as far south as Texas to winter feeding grounds.

Today, we know that bison seldom travel more than 320 kilometres (200 miles) during their migration. The bison that spend their summers feeding on open plains travel to wooded areas in winter. Those that summer on mountains, climb down into the valleys. Here, they find shelter among the trees and are protected from the worst of the icy winter storms.

Bison live an average of 25 years.

Group Lunch

What do bison eat? Most of their diet is made up of grasses such as wild oats, wild rye, wheat and speargrass. They also eat lichens, horsetails, vetches, blueberries, and bearberries.

Bison usually start to feed in early morning and munch away until dusk. They move around in a herd as they eat, keeping their muzzles close to the ground and tearing off tasty mouthfuls of grass.

Bison do not waste time chewing as they graze. Instead they store unchewed food in a special part of their stomach. When the bison has finished grazing, it looks for a resting spot out of the hot sun or cold winter winds. There it brings the unchewed food, or cud, back into its mouth and chews it in peace. Some bison chew their cud standing up, while others prefer to lie down and chew, chew, chew.

Time for lunch.

Snowplow Nose

In winter, the grass that the bison feeds on is covered by deep snow. But the bison is especially equipped to deal with this problem. It uses its large, flat nose as a built-in plow to shovel away the snow and uncover the grass. The bison pushes its nose through the snow, stopping at times to swing its head back and forth and sweep it away. The bison's nose is so effective that it can push away piles of snow more than one metre (3 feet) deep.

The bison's thick coat keeps it warm through the cold winter months.

Home on the Range

At one time, there were about 60 million bison
in North America. There were so many that if
they lined up in twos and walked past you, one
pair every minute, the parade would last almost
60 years. All these bison made their home on the
central plains of North America. They lived as
far north as Great Slave Lake in the Northwest
Territories and as far south as Mexico.

By 1900 these vast herds of bison were
almost wiped out. Only a few hundred bison
were left in all of North America. What
happened?

Lots of good eating here.

For centuries, the Plains Indians of North America had hunted the bison. But they hunted with spears, and killed relatively few. And they made use of every part of the animal: they used the hides to make tents and clothes, the meat for food, and the horns and bones to make tools.

But once European settlers came to North America, things changed very quickly. The settlers brought guns, which made it too easy to kill the bison. Soon there were almost no bison left in North America.

The bison often takes an afternoon siesta.

The Bison Come Back

By the early 1900s, people started to realize that hunting for bison should be stopped or soon even the few hundred remaining bison would be gone too. So concerned people created national parks where hunting bison was not permitted. Gradually, their numbers increased. Today, some 50,000 bison live in national parks scattered across the western prairies.

Enemy List

Before the early settlers came to North America, the Grizzly Bear, Mountain Lion and wolf were the major enemies of the bison. These predators usually attacked the very young or very old and sick bison. They did not often go after healthy adult bison. And for good reason. A bison has large hoofs and sharp horns to defend itself. And, a full-grown bison is so strong that it can run through a fence and even overturn a car.

Opposite page:

In order to feed in winter, bison must often clear away the snow using their heads and hoofs.

The More the Merrier

A lone bison is an unhappy bison. That is because the bison is a very social animal that likes to live and travel with other bison in a herd. The bison seem to know that there is safety in numbers. An enemy, such as a wolf, might be tempted to attack a single bison, but not a whole herd. Usually bison travel together in small groups of about 20. These small groups then sometimes get together to make a large herd. A herd can be made up of as many as 1000 bison.

Bison in a group usually do the same thing at the same time. When one bison wakes up at dawn and starts to graze, soon all the other bison in the herd begin to graze too. And when one bison lies down to chew its cud, the others soon follow suit. In a while the entire herd is chewing.

Stampede

Sometimes an odd noise will frighten a bison. Then, it might get nervous and start to run. Soon, all the other bison in the herd are racing around too. This momentary madness is called a stampede.

Stampedes can be very dangerous. Often the bison at the front of the stampede cannot stop or turn aside at an obstacle. If they stumble and fall they are trampled by the bison behind them. Indians used to use the stampede as a way of hunting bison. They would deliberately start a stampede and force the bison to run over a cliff. That way they could catch many bison at a time.

Mating Time

Bison mate in late summer and early fall. At that time, small groups of male bison, or bulls, join a large herd of female bison, or cows.

Once a bull finds a mate, it usually bellows like a foghorn in hopes of frightening away any rivals. Any bull foolhardy enough to ignore this loud warning is usually charged. When this happens, the two bulls rush toward each other until they collide. They often hit with such a powerful force that dirt flies from their fur. Fortunately, few ever get hurt. That is because the shaggy mane of hair on top of the bison's head softens the blow.

Sometimes, when two bulls charge at one another, they lock horns and have a shoving match, pushing each other back and forth. The winner of the match usually wins the female.

Bison cow.

A Baby is Born

In early summer, when food is plentiful, the cow gives birth. She often wanders a short way from her herd and picks a quiet spot—usually in a clump of trees—as her nursery. There, she gives birth to one baby bison, or "calf." Sometimes twins are born, but this is rare.

The newborn baby bison looks much like a baby cow, except that it is much stockier and its neck is shorter. Its eyes and ears are open, and its body is already covered with a fuzzy orange coat.

A tender touch.

Mother and Baby

The mother bison licks her baby very carefully as soon as it is born. Within minutes, the baby tries to stand up. Its legs are still weak and wobbly, and it usually collapses into a sprawling heap. But the baby tries again, and within about half an hour it is standing up by itself. In a few hours the baby may be running in circles around its mother.

For the first two or three days of its life, the calf stays close to its mother—away from the rest of the herd—sleeping and nursing on her milk. Even when mother and baby join the herd, the two are never far apart. Within a couple of weeks, the calf begins to play with the other calves in the herd. Soon it is spending most of the time with these young bison and only visits its mother once in a while to nurse.

That's close enough!

Big Babies

Even though a bison calf drinks its mother's milk until it is seven months old, it starts to nibble grass when it is one week old. With all this eating and playful exercise, the calf grows quickly.

By the time it is six weeks old, the bison calf is strong enough to knock a full-grown man off his feet. At eight weeks of age, the hump on its back and its horns start to grow. At first the horns are only tiny furred bumps. These do not reach adult size until the bison is eight years old.

By 10 weeks, the young bison's high-pitched baby squeal changes to a low deep grunty voice and its fur begins to grow darker. At 14 weeks, the young bison's coat is a dark chocolate brown.

The young bison now spends most of its time with the other young bison and less time with its mother. In fact, the young bison can often be found playing, grazing and sleeping together in the middle of the herd, while the adult bison stay on the outside.

Happy Birthday

By the time the young bison celebrates its first birthday, it weighs 180 kilograms (400 pounds) and its horns are 17 centimetres (7 inches) long. The time has come for the young bison to leave its mother. If it is male, it will join the other males in a small group. If it is female, it will become part of the big herd.

In about seven years, the bison will be ready to choose a mate of its own. Some bison have lived to be 40 years old in the wild, but most only live to be 20. During that time they will have several families, and their children and grandchildren will become part of the herd too.

Special Words

Bull   A male bison.

Calf   A baby bison.

Cow   A female bison.

Cud   Hastily swallowed food brought back for chewing by cud chewers such as deer, cows and bison.

Graze   To feed on growing grass.

Guard hairs   Long coarse hairs that make up the outer layer of the bison's coat.

Hoofs   Feet of cattle, deer, bison and some other animals.

Mate   To come together to produce young.

Migrate   To make regular annual trips in search of food.

Nurse   To drink the mother's milk.

Predator   Animal that lives by hunting others for food.

Wallow   The hollowed-out area caused when bison roll on the ground.

INDEX

Cover Photo: J.D. Markou (Valan Photos)

Photo Credits: Brian Milne (First Light Associated Photographs), pages 4, 14, 23; J.D. Taylor (Miller Services), page 7; Barry Ranford, pages 9, 45; Stephen J. Krasemann (Valan Photos), pages 10, 18, 24; Ron Watts (Miller Services), pages 12-13; Wayne Lankinen (Valan Photos), page 17; Parks Canada Photo Service, page 21; Tim Fitzharris (First Light Associated Photographers), pages 26, 42; Barry Griffiths (Network Stock Photo File), page 28; Hälle Flygare (Valan Photos), page 31; Thomas Kitchin (Valan Photos), page 32; Dennis Schmidt (Valan Photos), page 35; Harold Lambert (Miller Services), page 36; Esther Schmidt (Valan Photos), page 39; J.D. Markou (Valan Photos), page 40.

Getting To Know...

Nature's Children

OPOSSUM

Laima Dingwall

PUBLISHER	Joseph R. DeVarennes
PUBLICATION DIRECTOR	Kenneth H. Pearson
MANAGING EDITOR	Valerie Wyatt
SERIES ADVISOR	Merebeth Switzer
SERIES CONSULTANT	Michael Singleton
CONSULTANTS	Ross James
	Kay McKeever
	Dr. Audrey N. Tomera
ADVISORS	Roger Aubin
	Robert Furlonger
	Gaston Lavoie
EDITORIAL SUPERVISOR	Jocelyn Smyth
PRODUCTION MANAGER	Ernest Homewood
PRODUCTION ASSISTANTS	Penelope Moir
	Brock Piper
EDITORS	Katherine Farris Anne Minguet-Patocka
	Sandra Gulland Sarah Reid
	Cristel Kleitsch Cathy Ripley
	Elizabeth MacLeod Eleanor Tourtel
	Pamela Martin Karin Velcheff
PHOTO EDITORS	Bill Ivy
	Don Markle
DESIGN	Annette Tatchell
CARTOGRAPHER	Jane Davie
PUBLICATION ADMINISTRATION	Kathy Kishimoto
	Monique Lemonnier
ARTISTS	Marianne Collins Greg Ruhl
	Pat Ivy Mary Theberge

This series is approved and recommended by the Federation of Ontario Naturalists.

Canadian Cataloguing in Publication Data

Dingwall, Laima, 1953-
  Opossum

(Getting to know—nature's children)
Includes index.
ISBN 0-7172-1926-7

1. Opossums—Juvenile literature.
I. Title. II. Series.

QL737.M34D56 1985   j599.2   C85-098726-1

Have you ever wondered . . .

If you have ever seen an opossum, you have seen one of the most unusual animals in North America. What is so remarkable about the opossum, or possum as some people call it?

Well, to begin with, the opossum is the only animal in North America that hangs upside down by its tail. More than that, it has "hands" on its back legs, "feet" on its front legs, and it carries its babies in a pouch on its stomach. Read on to find out more about this odd, shy little creature which much prefers to be left alone.

Long white hairs cover the black-tipped fur below, giving the opossum a silvery look.

Where's Mom?

Opossum babies are very attached to their mother. They spend their first six weeks of life in a warm furry pouch on her stomach. And even after they leave the pouch for good, they like to be near their mother. Sometimes they even hitch a ride on her back when they get tired.

But these three youngsters are old enough to be on their own. What is in store for them? Read on to find out.

Relatives Near and Far

If you could hop aboard a time machine and travel back 200 million years to the age of the dinosaurs, you would probably see the tiny opossum scurrying between the legs of the mighty Brontosaurus. There are no dinosaurs around today, but the opossum is still here.

The opossum belongs to a very ancient group of animals called the marsupials. Besides being old-timers, marsupials have something else in common. The female carries her babies in a fur-lined pouch on her belly.

The common, or Virginia Opossum, is the only marsupial that lives in North America. Scientists believe it traveled up from South America millions of years ago. The early Indians gave it the name we know today. They called it ''apasum,'' which means white animal.

Several opossum relatives still live in Mexico and Central and South America, but perhaps the most famous marsupials of all live in Australia. They are the kangaroo, wallaby, wombat, Tasmanian devil and the teddybear look-alike koala.

Opossum Country

Most North American opossums live in the warm southeastern parts of the United States. But in the last 100 years or so, opossums have started to move north into the New England states and southern Canada. Opossums can even be found as far west as California, Oregon, Washington and southern British Columbia.

Opossums often live on the edge of a forest or on farmlands. They do not stray far from a stream or marsh. Some opossums have even moved into suburbs, towns and cities, where they usually set up home in parks.

Opossums often climb up trees to escape from their enemies.

Sizing Up the Opossum

Imagine a white rat as big as a house cat. That is what the opossum looks like. A full-grown male opossum weighs as much as six kilograms (12 pounds), or about as much as a fat cat. From the tip of its nose to the end of its tail it measures 60 to 80 centimetres (24-32 inches). Female opossums are slightly smaller.

Bless My Whiskers

The opossum has four rows of cat-like whiskers—each about eight centimetres (3 inches) long—growing out from the sides of its nose and cheeks. And just like a cat's whiskers, the opossum's whiskers are sensitive feelers. This is especially important when the opossum is wandering through brush at night, in search of food. If it can get its head through a narrow opening without its whiskers touching, then the opossum knows it can probably squeeze the rest of its body through too.

Opossum Picnic

When it is hungry, the opossum keeps its round, pink nose close to the ground so that it can sniff out its dinner quickly. It will eat almost anything that flies, crawls, hops or even walks by.

Its favorite foods are insects, especially crickets, grasshoppers, beetles and butterflies. But it will also eat small animals such as earthworms, snails, salamanders, frogs and lizards. Even snakes are considered a tasty treat! An opossum on the prowl will raid birds' nests to feast on the eggs or young birds, and it will also hunt mice, moles, young rabbits and squirrels. In the city, the opossum often knocks over garbage cans and digs up vegetable gardens looking for food.

"Oh dear—a dead end."

The opossum also eats fruit and plants. It will gorge on berries and other fruit that have fallen to the ground, and if it is still hungry, it will climb trees in search of more. Opossums that live in the south particularly enjoy persimmons and pokeberries. And it is common to see them feeding on grasses, clover, seeds and nuts.

If there is lots of food available, an opossum's home range might only be as big as five hectares (12 acres). But during lean times it may wander over an area four times that big looking for food.

An apple's a treat that's hard to beat.

Fuzzy Fur

Most of the opossum's body is covered with a double-thick fur coat. The white outercoat of stiff, finger-length guard hair helps to keep the opossum dry. The inner coat of thick, short hair is warm and woolly. It traps in body heat. This inner coat can either be pure white or white tipped with black. The mixture of white and black fur gives the opossum its silvery gray color.

Like a cat, the opossum uses its rough tongue to groom its coat. First it licks its front paws clean and uses them to scrub its face. Then it usually sits on its haunches and gives its belly a good cleaning.

This untidy fellow is in need of a good grooming.

Double Grip

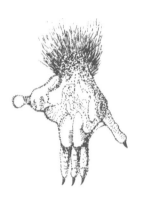

Rear paw

Imagine having your hands where your feet are and feet where your hands are. That may sound backwards to you, but the opossum finds it very useful.

The opossum has a thumb on each of its back paws which means it can grip things the way you can with your hands. Having a thumb is a terrific help to a tree climber whose safety depends on hanging on. The opossum also has an extra "hand." Its tail can wrap around a branch while the opossum is high up in a tree, leaving its hands free to grab the next branch.

Getting up and down trees is no problem either. The opossum has long sharp claws on all of its fingers and toes, except its thumbs. It digs these claws into the tree bark for a good safe grip.

Hanging Around

The opossum is the only animal in North America that can hang upside down by its tail. Why it does this is not known. But it is easy to see how it does it. It simply wraps its tail around a tree branch and lets go with its hands.

If you see an opossum hanging upside down by its tail, you can be sure it is a young opossum. Full-grown opossums are too fat and heavy to hang from their tails. If they tried it—BONK—they would probably land head first on the ground.

"Look mom . . . no hands . . . or feet!"

Opossum on the Run

If you ran a race against an opossum, who would win? Probably you would. The fastest time ever recorded for an opossum was only 13 kilometres (8 miles) an hour.

But even if you could outrun an opossum, you probably would not be able to catch it. The opossum is built so low to the ground that it can easily duck under bushes and shrubs, squeeze into small holes in the ground, scurry into hollow logs, hide behind piles of rocks or even nip up a tree to avoid you.

A walking opossum is a real slowpoke. It has a plodding gait that looks awkward because it moves the two legs on the same side at the same time.

There are lots of good hiding places in this dense cover.

Opossum Hideaway

Opossums do not spend a lot of time and energy digging a den or building a home for themselves. Instead, they take over a burrow abandoned by a groundhog or skunk or move into a hollow log or even the hollow of a tree. In the city, an opossum might make its home under a house porch, in a garage or even inside a storm sewer.

Once it has moved in, the opossum lines its den with plenty of leaves and twigs for comfort and warmth. How does the opossum carry this bedding home? First, it gathers leaves in its front feet and pushes them under its body. Then it wraps its long, flexible tail around the leaves, picks them up and hurries home, carrying the load of leaves with its tail.

When its den is finished the opossum snoozes away the days in it.

Bundle Up!

The opossum is not built to withstand frosty weather. The bottoms of its feet are bare and so are its long, thin ears. And, except for a few stiff bristles, its tail is naked too. This is not a problem for opossums that live in warm climates, but what about those that have moved into cold-weather country?

If the weather gets really cold, an opossum spends up to two weeks at a stretch snuggled up in its den. It does not go out to search for food. Instead it lives off a thick layer of body fat that it built up by eating an extra lot in the fall. But in a long cold spell, the opossum must go out and look for food. Brrr! Many northern opossums have lost the tips of their ears and the end of their tails because of frostbite.

During winter an opossum may have to risk frostbite in order to get a drink.

"Playing Possum"

Owls, foxes and bobcats are just a few of the animals that consider opossums a tasty meal. To avoid these enemies, an opossum will often run for a safe hiding spot or up a tree. But as we have seen, opossums are not fast runners. So, to fool their pursuers, the opossum has come up with another trick. It flops over and plays dead. Since none of its enemies will eat a dead animal, the opossum often saves itself.

If you are ever lucky enough to see an opossum play dead, or ''play possum,'' as it is sometimes called, here is what you would see. When the enemy gets too close, the opossum topples over on its side, lets its mouth drop open and often closes its eyes. It even slows down its breathing and its heartrate. The opossum acts so lifeless that it will not budge or even flicker its eyes if its enemy pokes it or picks it up in its mouth and shakes it.

However, sometimes the opossum gets mixed up. If the predator puts it back on the ground on the wrong side, it will forget it is supposed to be dead and flip over onto the other side. So much for playing dead!

This Opossum Means Business

If an opossum is cornered by an enemy and does not have a chance to "play possum," it may try to frighten off the attacker. It faces its enemy, opens its mouth wide to show off its sharp teeth and hisses and growls loudly.

The opossum even makes itself look bigger than it really is by standing up as tall as possible and holding its tail straight up. The sight of such a fierce-looking opossum is often enough to make most of its enemies think twice.

"Come any closer and you'll be sorry!"

Mating Time

The opossum is a loner and usually chooses to live by itself. The only time that adult opossums can be seen together is during mating season. When an opossum mates depends on where it lives. Opossums that live in the south mate from January to August. More northerly opossums mate between February and August.

Opossums usually mate only once during the mating season. But sometimes a female opossum may mate twice and have two litters in one season—the first in late February and the second in late July.

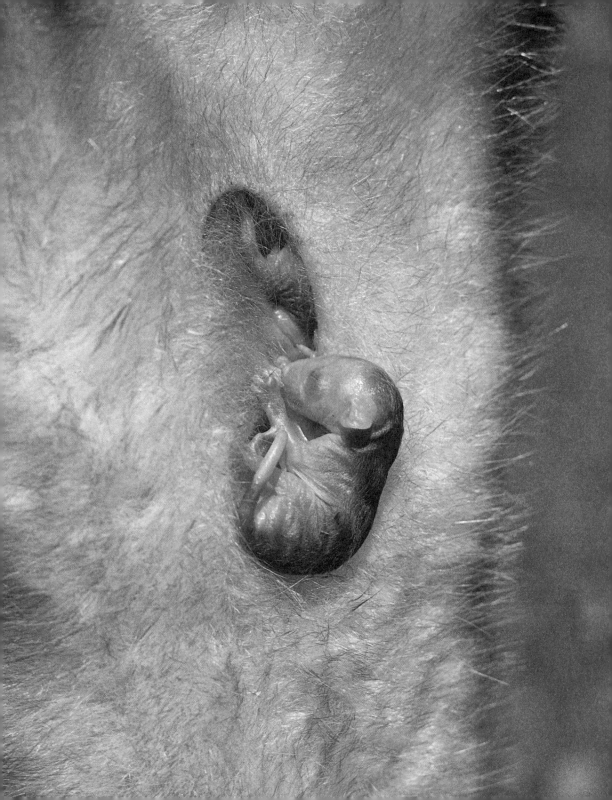

A Cozy Nursery

Just 13 days after mating, the female opossum is ready to give birth. She lines her den with plenty of leaves and twigs to make a cozy nursery. There she gives birth to as many as 20 babies at one time. She raises her babies alone, without any help from the male.

You could easily hold an entire litter of 20 opossums in a tablespoon! The newborn opossum measures just 14 millimetres (half an inch) long from one end to the other. That is about the same size as a honeybee.

The newborn opossum is rosy pink and hairless. Its ears and eyes are still closed and its back legs and tail are small stubs. But its front legs are well developed and come equipped with claws.

Everyone into the Pouch, Please

The first few moments of a baby opossum's life are quite busy. As soon as it is born, the mother opossum licks it very carefully. Next she licks her own stomach fur to make it moist and slippery. The baby, using the tiny claws on its front feet as mini-hooks, wriggles and squirms its way along this slippery path until it finds the fur-lined pouch on its mother's stomach. Then it crawls in.

With so many young it's quite a tight squeeze.

Home Sweet Pouch

The mother opossum's stomach pouch is like a big, warm, woolly pocket. She can open her pocket whenever she likes by simply relaxing her muscles and close it again by tightening them.

Hidden inside this pouch are 13 nipples arranged in the shape of a horseshoe. There are 12 nipples along the edge and one nipple in the centre.

Even though the opossum mother sometimes gives birth to as many as 20 babies at once, she can only feed 13. There is one nipple for one baby. Those that do not find a nipple do not survive.

Each newborn struggles to latch onto one of the mother's nipples.

Growing Up Inside a Pouch

Once inside its mother's pouch, the newborn opossum finds a nipple and immediately starts to drink its mother's rich milk. It will not let go of this nipple for about 60 days.

The baby grows very quickly, and life inside the pouch gets more and more crowded. About 14 days after birth, the baby starts to grow fuzzy, silvery fur. Its back legs and tail grow longer and stronger, and it gains weight steadily. But, it is not until the baby opossum opens its eyes—between the ages of 58 and 72 days—that it becomes curious about the outside world. It is only then that it lets go of the nipple and finally pokes its head outside the pouch.

This young opossum may live up to seven years.

Hello There, World!

Once out of the pouch, the baby opossum is still weak and quite helpless. And although it starts to explore the world, it does not stray far from its mother. Because its legs are still rather wobbly, it often rides piggy-back style, clinging with its tiny, but strong, claws to its mother's back.

Traveling this way, the mother takes all her babies out on short trips from the nest. During these outings, she shows them how to find food and climb trees.

"I'll get the hang of this yet!"

Moving Out

The baby opossum nurses until it is about 100 days old. When it is hungry, it just climbs into its mother's pouch and latches onto a nipple. Sometimes, if the mother is lying on her side sunning herself, the baby opossum hangs backwards out of the pouch and suns itself too, without letting go of the nipple.

The baby opossum grows and learns quickly. By the time it is 100 days old, it is ready to leave its mother and find a den of its own. Usually it does not wander far from its mother's den. But although it lives nearby, the young opossum does not spend time with its mother or brothers and sisters. Now it prefers to be on its own. When it is about eight months old it will be ready to mate and start a family of its own.

Special Words

Den   Animal home.

Groom   To clean.

Guard hair   Long coarse hairs that make up the outer layer of an opossum's coat.

Home range   The area where an opossum looks for food.

Marsh   An area where the ground is soaked with water.

Marsupials   A family of animals whose females carry the young in a pouch until they are fully developed.

Mate   To come together to produce young.

Mating season   The time of year during which animals mate.

Muscles   Parts of the animal's body that help it move.

Nipple   The part of the mother's body through which a baby drinks her milk.

Pouch   The fur-lined pocket on the female marsupial where the babies live until they are developed.

Predator   An animal that lives by hunting other animals.

INDEX

Cover Photo: Steve Maslowski

Photo Credits: Karl H. Maslowski, pages 4, 7, 36, 39, 40; Steve Maslowski, pages 16, 19, 23, 27, 28, 43, 44; R.C. Simpson (Valan Photos), pages 8, 31, 35; Leonard Lee Rue IV (Miller Services), pages 11, 32; H.R. Hungerford, pages 12, 15, 21; Ontario Ministry of Natural Resources, page 24.